The Poetic Heart of God

By

Sophia Nicole Benton

First published by AuthorHouse 01/10/2006

ISBN: 1-4184-6699-9 (e-book)
ISBN: 1-4184-4535-5 (Paperback)

Library of Congress Control Number: 2004091001

This book is printed on acid free paper.

Printed in the United States of America
Bloomington, IN

The Poetic Heart of God is a God sent message of the hour. It reflects the wisdom Sophia N. Benton has gleaned from being before the Lord in her life and ministry. The Poetic Heart of God is a book, which will add proper perspective to every believer. The value of her God sent material is inestimable. The message of this book can spell the difference between life and death for some believers.

This is a must for any Christian who is in search of balance and stability when dealing with the thorns of life. I would urge every growing Christian to take the time to read it.

Charles E. Lewis, Sr., MCE
Pastor
Antioch UHC

A Pastor After God's Own Heart

Why did I title this the way that I did
A Pastor After God's Own Heart
Because some of the things we put him through
Another would probably have had to depart.

Just like little children
We sometimes go astray
But yet you are always there
To direct us back to the right way.
We thank you for not letting us slide
Most of all, we thank you for being our model guide.

Sometimes we get entangled in some things
That we know we should not be
But yet you are always right there
To speak a word that loose the chains
And allows us to go free.
We thank you for being a corrector
Most of all, we thank you for being our protector.

Sometimes like sheep
We get stubborn-stricken and don't want what we
need
Like chastisement or being pulled back from unseen
danger to the path that is right—oh no, sometimes we
would rather put up a fight
And to think, you are still up battling for us against the
enemy in the wee hours of the night.

We thank you for not giving up on us even though it
would have been our very own disaster
But most of all, we thank you for being our dedicated
Pastor!

Not to forget those times
You have been preaching away
And our faces at one point or another
Are screaming, "Lord, not today!"
But you confidently and boldly stood to proclaim what
God told you to say
We thank you for not quitting but continuing to preach
the Word
But most of all, we thank you for being a Shepherd of
this herd.

You are anointed and appointed
For such a time as this, and through it all we extend
our love
For we know that you are truly God-sent directly from
above.

Once again we say thank you and you are
appreciated more than you know
For all your efforts and all the many things you do
For we are truly blessed to have an awesome Pastor
such as you!

We love you!

A Pastor After God's Own Heart (enlightened)

To my Pastors, I can truly say you both lead the flock to safety. You chasten the ones who rebel against God's Word because of the love you have for God's people. You both labor consistently and unconditionally. You feed, protect, guide, and nourish those in which God has placed under your covering. There are no others that could ever fulfill your ministry and do the job as well as you two do together. I love you both with the love of Christ and may God's choice blessing overtake you.

Jeremiah 3:15: "And I will give you shepherds according to my heart, and they will feed you with knowledge and understanding."

A Woman of Power

Min. Lewis, you are a woman of great worth
Who has taught us a lot of things
Pure, noble, honest, and true
Are just some of the virtues that you bring.

You've instilled in us the Word of God
And have taught the way that things should be
Then you've toiled and labored with us
To help us reach our predestined destiny.

We are forever grateful
For the many ways you are a blessing to us all
We give you a standing ovation
And we give to you much applause.

We want you to know
We love you from the heart
And in each of our lives
You've played an awesome part.

May God richly bless
Everything you put forth your hands to do
For only His repayment could fulfill
The honor which you're due.

A Woman of Power (enlightened)

Behind every great man there is a mighty woman who helped to push and to encourage and also to minister unto him in the darkest of hours. You have helped to build him up and to war off the attacks of the enemy. To add to being a helpmeet to your spouse comes the responsibility of being a mother, a counselor, a friend, and a dynamic teacher of the Word of God. You are a strong woman, and I marvel at your strength and your God-given ability to minister His Word. You are forever in my prayers!

Proverbs 31:10-12: "Who can find a virtuous wife? For her worth is far above rubies. The heart of her husband safely trusts her; So she will have no lack of gain. She does him good and not evil all the days of her life."

All for His Glory

How do I come to say
All of the pains that come my way
Lord, my heart seems to be
Filled with stress and agony
But whenever I really want to talk
It seems like everyone turns away and walks
Lord, you are my only hope
For by myself I cannot cope
I am tired, Master, please take my hand
No one else seems to understand
My heart is heavy laden and tears I cry
More and more pain as time goes by
Yet in my deepest hurts that cannot actually be seen
I am forever naked before you and upon thy Word I lean
Though the pressure is on, I can still hear your voice
That alone gives me reason to rejoice
For you said in your Word
You would never leave me nor forsake
On the cross at Calvary this pain you did take
So I cast this burden off of me
I shall begin to shout with the voice of victory
I will put on the garment of high praise
Remembering at your command the very dead can be raised
I surrender all my troubles
Over to you
That I may come out
Giving you the glory you're due
You are truly worthy
Of all the glory

For you allowed me to stand the test of life
Just to proclaim my story
For every trial you've brought me through
For every truth I never knew
For every tear you've wiped from my eye
For not allowing me to believe the devil's lie
For every time you allowed me to triumph over the enemy
For allowing your Son to die at Calvary
I just want to say thank you
I greatly magnify your Name
In knowing you, Lord
My life shall never be the same!

All for His Glory (enlightened)

I have seen some weary days. I have had a lot of trials and tribulations within my life. Age has absolutely nothing to do with trouble, heartache, or sadness. Misery does not have any prejudices, and it loves company. We, the body of Christ, must make up in our minds that we will not settle for what the enemy has to offer. There is a better way. You may go through hard times and you may suffer loss every now and then, but you must know that all that you go through is for a purpose. There is a valid reason behind all that you are going through. You may not see it right now, but if you hold onto the Word of God, God's Glory shall be seen. Whenever you want to get the best out of a particular object, you sometimes have to press hard and long, sometimes a crushing may have to take place. Whenever you squeeze an orange, you get orange juice. Whenever you dry out grapes, you get raisins. Whenever you crush coal, you get a diamond. You are God's diamond and this crushing that you are going through is for His Glory. Do not lose hope. Do not be discouraged. God is setting you up for your next level! He wants to manifest Himself to you in a way you have never seen before. You can make it! This storm will pass, and you shall be filled with the Glory of the Lord!

2 Corinthians 4:8-10: "We are hard pressed on every side, yet not crushed; we are perplexed, but not in despair; persecuted, but not forsaken; struck down, but not destroyed—always carrying the Lord Jesus, that the life of Jesus also may be manifested in our body."

Arise, God Is Calling Your Name

One person can do but so much
God has lives out here that only I can touch
I have to learn to lay aside every weight
For there are lost souls waiting on me for the kingdom's sake
God, help me to strengthen thou feeble knees
Help me to stand strong and tall and to stop looking for the next person
To fulfill that for which I've been called
My Lord, My God, I say
Who am I that you should send lost souls my way?
I, my Lord, am a twisted mess
And you want me to go out and confess
Confess and proclaim the Holy Word
Just the thought alone makes the feeling absurd
Surely, Lord, I am not the one you're looking for
I'm not pure enough; I'm not anointed enough, need I say more?
"Enough, my child, all of your excuses I've heard
You are not here by mistake
Don't deny My Word
Your strength comes directly from Me
You are a mighty servant of Mine
You have the power to make the devil flee
It is a faith factor, and you must study My Word and seek My face
You have all that you need, and I will not exempt you that another will take your place
Put off the old man and cast away fear
I've placed life in you, and by My Word you will adhere

But I give you a choice, it's up to you to seek Me and stand
To find out what you are truly called to do
I do not want the blood of My people upon your hands
Then I will have to deal with you
So arise, My servant, and take My hand
I've given you My Word to enable you to stand
And all because I love you and I genuinely do care
I will not put more on you than you are able to bare
Stay in My Word, devour it, consume it, hide it in your heart, and build yourself up in Me
Watch and pray as you allow My hands to unfold and you will see
You have the ability of being all that I've created you to be
There is no reason, no reason at all
That you should not fulfill this heavenly call
Open your spiritual eyes that you may see
You have nothing to fear as you walk into your destiny."

Arise, God Is Calling Your Name (enlightened)

The cool of the day has come. God is now walking through the garden of your heart asking the question, "Where are you?" Why are you trying to hide from the things of God? What is it that you are trying to keep Him from seeing? Are you naked in some areas of your life and don't want Him to see you uncovered? Are you trying to sew a little bit of prayer and a little bit of praise together to keep eyes off of you? God knows you, and He knows you by name. You know God has been calling you for sometime now. You need to answer the call. There are some lost souls out there waiting on you to come by and speak life into them. It is time-out for doing the things that you want to do and doing the things that you feel are important. God has called you into the ministry for such a time as this, and He should be first priority on your list. If you do not know clearly what that ministry is, pray and seek the Lord for an answer. You will be judged on whether or not you did what you were commissioned to do while here on earth. Your ministry could be singing, and if so, sing to the Glory of God and stop trying to entertain folk. Your ministry may be preaching, and if so, preach the pure, unadulterated Word of God and not what man wants to hear. Your ministry may be to play on the instruments of God, and if so, make music unto the Lord. You may have a street ministry, and if so, go even if you have to go alone and not when everyone is looking. Whatever your hands find to do, do it to God's Glory! Arise, go forth, and do the work that the Lord ordained for you to do before the foundation of the world!

Genesis 3:9: "And the Lord God called to Adam and said to him, Where are you?"

Awesome God

Lord, that I may know you
In the power of your resurrection
That I may walk in your wisdom
And follow the light of your direction
Your Word, oh Lord, is a light unto my path
And a lamp unto my feet
It brightens the darkest parts in my life
Your word protects me from defeat
Who is like my God
Who sits high on His throne
No one has ever walked in such power
No one has ever known
Such wisdom, such grace
Such an awesome God
We dare not attempt to behold your face
You are my majesty
You hold my destiny
I do not worry
Because you're in control
I do not fret
For my life you hold
All glory and honor
I give unto YOU
I bow in my spirit
To give you the reverence you're due!

Awesome God (enlightened)

There is not a word in the human dictionary that could describe my God. If I had to choose just a few words, they would be words like *indescribable*, *overwhelming*, *breathtaking*, *mind-blowing*, *inconceivable*, *miraculous*, *phenomenal*, *non-conforming*, *peculiar*, and the list goes on and on! Is there anybody who can identify with me that Jehovah is just GOD? There is none like Him. There is nothing and no one that can be compared to Him. Before the world was formed, He was. After this world is over, yet will He be!

Revelation 1:8: "'I am Alpha and Omega, the Beginning and the End, the First and the Last,' says the Lord, 'who is and who was and who is to come, the Almighty.'"

Broken but Not Destroyed

Pieces of my very life
Shattered, crushed, and ruined
Fragments lying everywhere
My God, My God, what are you doing?

A state of confusion
Is where I am about to be
A spirit of frustration
Is trying to rest on me.

Dark clouds all around
Frustrated, perplexed, and anxious I am
Yet a still sweet voice says,
Peace! For I've already sent my Sacrificial Lamb.

The blood that dripped down
From His head to His feet
Can wash away all of your pains
And lift you up from defeat.

Arise, I hear the Lord say,
My daughter and my son this shall no longer be
For your anguish Christ hung upon a tree.

Your victory is here
He that Is, Was, and Is to come
Lives in you so every battle you've won.

Lift up your head
And be ye lifted up
That the Lord God on high
May forever fill your cup!

Broken but Not Destroyed (enlightened)

Have you ever had something that was broken, and you pieced it back together again? No matter how well you super-glued it, you could probably still tell where the cracks were. Sometimes in this walk of life we become broken. We may have become broken in relationships, careers, finances, or even our dreams. Yet, in our broken state, if we would just allow God to come in and piece us back together again, we would be better than we were before. No one would be able to tell where we were broken or what caused the breaking. In our broken state, it is then that we can see God's work in our lives clearer. If it was not for our pit experiences, we would not be able to appreciate God as we do. In our hard afflictions, we then learn the ways of the Lord. Paul said it best in Romans 8:18: "For I reckon that the sufferings of this present time is not to be compared with the glory which shall be revealed in us."

Call on Him

Sometimes I feel
I cannot go on
Sometimes I feel
I am all alone

But when I think
Of how I've been blessed
I find peace with myself
And then I can rest

When I need a friend
To guide me through
I call on JESUS
To turn my gray clouds blue

Jesus is my friend
And He is yours, too
What He has done for me
He will also do for you!

Call on Him (enlightened)

We sometimes get so caught up with the cares of this world, and when trouble arises, we call on everyone except the Name of the Lord. It is imperative that we realize that "folk" cannot deliver us. We may have a pity party with them and allow them to make our flesh feel better, but true deliverance comes from wailing out to God and telling Him that you surrender and you need His power and His anointing to be manifested in your life. All you have to do is call on Him and He will answer you.

Jeremiah 33:3: "Call unto Me and I will answer thee and show thee great and mighty things which thou knowest not."

Children of God Are <u>Precious</u> in His Sight!

What would God
have to say about you?
Except He sees you
as faithful and true.

You are a powerful creation
that has been ordained from on high
and the more you stay in God's presence
greater anointing you shall receive as time goes by.

Never doubt the things
God has called you to
for while you were yet in your mother's womb
He had already charged these things for you to do.

To do His will
without doubt or fear
Walking hand in hand with your **Father**
He wants you to know that He is near.

He is closer to you than you know
Don't you realize it was He
Every time the storms would rise
He'd speak a word and calm your sea.

When the road would get tough
and you were not sure
He'd take you under His wings
to allow you to know He's got you secure.

You are anointed and appointed by God
You truly know His voice
Do not let the obstacles of this life
Shake your faith and get you off course.

You are His chosen vessel
Fearfully and wonderfully made
For if it had been for you and you alone
His Son, He still would have gave.

Go forth my daughter of Zion, go forth my son
Think not back into the past
For we know it is only what we
Do for Christ that shall last.

A new birthing in your spirit shall come
You shall walk as you never have before
With the very confidence of the Almighty God
For you are now standing under heaven's open door.

Spiritual blessings are being decreed over you
By faith you shall never lack again
For the mouth of God has declared in your life
No more defeat, no more struggle; He has equipped
You to Win!

Walk in your liberty
Where-in Christ has set you free
That you may let the enemy know
You shall be all that Christ created you to be.

Rejoice in the Spirit
Go on and be exceedingly glad
For on this day and this very hour
You have just made the devil mad.

But so what; he is mad but without power
For he is under your Daddy's authority
Therefore you shall walk
In total, complete victory!

Children of God Are Precious in His Sight (enlightened)

Regardless of what others have to say about you and despite what you may or may not have done in your past, you are still precious in the sight of God. He loves you unconditionally, and you are valuable to Him. You are a product directly from the mouth of God. If He took the time to speak you into existence, know that He has greater things in store for your life. You may be feeling like a complete failure. You may be experiencing a sense of void in your life, and you are trying to fill it, but you just can't. You may have had some setbacks in life, and you feel there is no hope. You may have had to face disappointment after disappointment, and the more you pray, the more the devil turns up the heat. You are in this particular place at this particular time because God has something great in store for your life. It does not matter what you did yesterday. We need to stop trying to hold God's people to yesterday's mess-ups! We have all made a mess at some point in our lives. I encourage every reader to arise and continue in the grace of God. You are special to Him, and He wants you to know that there is nothing you can do to make Him stop loving you. See yourself as God sees you! Keep looking up, for God's grace is looking down.

1 Corinthians 2:2: "For I determined to know anything among you except Jesus Christ and Him crucified."

The Word Is Deadly Poison to the Enemy

Take for instance you have this mouse
And he continues to squeak all around in your house
You put out poison that he may eat
And to you it looks as though he's having a feast
And on tomorrow he comes back around to find
There's nothing more than cheese mixed with poison
To be found
You allow the mouse to eat and eat
Then he curls on his back for this is the day of defeat
This is just the same with your situations in life
The devil comes to kill, steal, and to destroy
Yet the Word on the inside of you is poison that you
May use to put an end to this war
It is a repeated cycle that we must do
Every day confess the Word boldly for it is faithful and
true
Do not look at what it looks like
For that has nothing to do with God; His word is a
Lamp unto our path and allows us to see
And if you use it like He has instructed, the devils you
Confront will have to flee
They may flee for a while, right out of your spiritual
Door, then the Lord shall kill them one by one and
Those devils will be seen no more. Therefore, don't
Get discouraged because it doesn't happen when you
Think, and don't take your eyes off of Jesus and His
Word for then like Peter you will begin to sink. Stay
Focused on the Lord that you may stay afloat and
When the designated time comes, God will bid you out
Of the boat.

The Word Is Deadly Poison to the Enemy (enlightened)

The enemy may look like he is winning from time to time. Yes, I know that your situation is bad, and it looks like it is impossible for life to be breathed back into your situation. However, God is a God of impossibilities. Trust God! When your back is up against a wall and you know that the enemy desires to wipe you out and you are convinced that if God does not come to see about you the enemy will destroy you, well now is the time to open your mouth and begin to travail, and He will step in right on time. God did it for Daniel in the lion's den, and surely He is the same God now that He was back then. If God made a way for the children of Israel at the Red Sea, surely He can be a bridge in your situation. If God can deliver the three Hebrew boys out of the fiery furnace, certainly He can bring you through whatever you are facing. God has given us the authority and the license through the Name of Jesus that we may be conquerors and not overthrown by the enemy.

John 10:10: "The enemy comes to kill, steal and to destroy but God came to give life and life more abundantly."

The Devil's Testimony

I bow down and give thanks to me
for you have not accepted Christ

I bow down and give thanks
for I the trickster rule your life

I bow down and give thanks
for you are blind and can not see

I bow down and give thanks
for you will not use the power God has given
you to charge me to flee

I bow down and give thanks
for you will not accept although you've heard

All you have to do is accept Jesus Christ
and His living word

I bow down and give thanks
for you think you are okay

Even if I were you
I would know to go the other way

But no you stay like you are
I would love to make hell your home

For eternity you shall be with me
Enduring fire and brimstone

I do not love you I don't even care
Can't you see?
I only want someone to share _my_ agony

Hell has enlarged herself
I've got room for plenty more

That is why I am always right there
Knocking at your door

The door of your heart
But yet that Jesus is too

Therefore you have a choice
It is completely up to you

You stand at a crossroad
And I'll tell you Jesus loves you
And if you choose Him I must go

For I can not stay where Christ resides
Even that I know

So who I ask you a question
Who will it be
Will you keep allowing me
To control your life continually?
Or will you use wisdom
And choose Christ as your final destiny?

The choice is yours!!

The Devil's Testimony (enlightened)

Have you ever taken the time to think about what the devil is saying about you and the things that he brings before you to entice you with. Have you ever thought about how it is after you have given in to that trickster the bad feeling you get and how you are convicted in your heart and how he makes you feel like you are low down and dirty. Yet on the other hand Jesus is standing before God pleading your case and asking God to forgive you and to give you another chance. The devil cares nothing about you. All he wants you to do is to give in to his wicked schemes that are well strategized and presented to you in a very appealing way. He only wants to entrap you as well as me and to try to present us guilty before God. He only wants you to use your body, soul and mind for the nonprofitable things of the world. God is a God of love and there is hope if you would only believe the words of Christ. Do not believe the lies of the enemy. Do not be a part of the testimony of the devil any longer. God wants to deliver you and to set you free from every trickery of the enemy. You have to want it for yourself. Hell was not created for you. It was only created for the devil and his imps. You do not have to die and go to hell. The choice is yours. God is calling out to you today. This may be the last chance you get. Tomorrow is not promised to you. If you die right now are you sure that you will go and be with God in heaven. If you can not answer "yes" to that question without doubt this message is for you. God wants to save you right now. New life can be yours if you just confess the Lord Jesus and believe in your heart. Turn your back on the devil and go full-fledge for Christ! Salvation is a gift from God and it is free-you can't get any better than that! Will you accept Christ today?

Therefore Sheol has enlarged itself and opened its mouth beyond measure; Their glory and their multitude and their pomp and he who is jubilant, shall descend into it. Isaiah 5:14

Desert Storm

When you find yourself in the wilderness to revive your spirit from the
rough winds blowing, dust storms all around
Just the Master, Holy Spirit, and yourself
No one will have a pity party for you
Trials, tribulations, and misfortunes all around
Now you are in your desert storm
Yet the Word of God shall stand and never die
Take time out in time of tribulations
Just to say thank you
Not to ask for deliverance out of your storm but help to go through until the end.
Afterwards when the storm is over
rejoicing is birthed and trials are swallowed up in Victory
Your spirit-man has increased and your anointing is overflowing
Desert storm is the best place to learn how much faith you really have in God
God will see you through only if you are willing to trust Him
He will not leave you alone
There is peace in the midst of the storm.

Desert Storm (enlightened)

Life sometimes can throw you a fastball, and it seems like every time you swing you miss. You cannot pray the right prayer; you cannot sing the right song; you feel as though God is so far away from you, and all you want to do is feel His presence in your life once again. You just do not feel deliverance is coming. Nothing is going right, and you just want to throw in the towel. Remember, we do not live by feelings or by what we see. We were created to walk by faith and not by sight. I do not care how bad the enemy is trying to get you to give up and quit, if you just hold on, your change will come. God is getting ready to release your blessings. You are too close to give up now! You have given too much of yourself to call it a defeated battle. You are getting ready to experience a turning in your spirit and an unction from the Holy Spirit deep down in your soul. God is speaking to you right now. He is saying, don't give up, you can make it, I am with you, keep the faith, and just hold on. Trouble does not last always, and God has already promised you the victory!

Psalms 30:5: "Weeping may endure for a night, but joy cometh in the morning."

Do You Want To Be Used?

God is a Spirit
And yes it is true
If you avail yourself to Him
He can use you too.

Age does not matter
God just needs a human vessel to yield
That He may place that very one
Upon the battlefield

One thing you must remember
And that is you cannot rely
On flesh to lead your way
And His temple you must not defile

Come out from among them
Who influence you to go astray
That you may do the will of God
Each and every day.

Do You Want To Be Used? (enlightened)

Ministry does not come with natural age. God looks at the growth of a person's spirit and the pureness of his heart towards Him. If you have a heart that wants nothing more than to please God and you are willing to serve in all capacities, you are fit for his service. Do not look at who is looking at you in the natural focus on heaven and pleasing your Father in glory. Know this, when you minister, you are doing it for Christ not men.

Colossians 3:23-25: "And whatever you do, do it heartily, as unto the Lord and not to men, knowing that from the Lord you will receive the reward of the inheritance; for you serve the Lord Jesus Christ. But he who does wrong will be repaid for what he has done, and there is no partiality."

Don't Cry...Smile

Our loved one
Has now gone on
He is in
His new heavenly home
That is a blessing,
To some in disguise
But the Lord says, "My Child, don't cry...smile."

Smile when you think of
How it used to be
When you look back at how
You have all those precious memories.

Smile when you think of
How he brightened up your day
With his funny jokes
And his very unique ways.

And then be thankful to God
For giving him to us
For just a little while
As you can almost hear Larry say
Don't cry for me...smile.

Don't cry for me
For I've done what you all have to do
Just make sure you're ready
When it is time for you to move.

I knew that my end was near
Now I am at peace
For I've gone the last mile
Therefore rejoice
Don't cry…smile.

I have no more sickness
I have no more pain
Now all I see is sunshine
For God has washed away my rain.

I am better off now
Than I was before
I was glad when I heard Jesus
Knocking at my heart's door.

Yes, I have gone my last mile
So don't you cry, wipe your weeping eyes and
Smile.

In loving memory of Larry Baker

Don't Cry...Smile (enlightened)

We as God's people are just passing by on this earth. This world is not our eternal home. Sometimes God shows just how much He loves His children here on earth when He calls them unto Himself to place them into their heavenly home. God knows what is best, and we can be reassured even in the difficult times of losing a loved one that His perfected will has still been done. He is not a God of mistakes. Continue to praise God in the good and the bad, the happy and the sad.

1 Corinthians 15:51-53: "Behold, I tell you a mystery: We shall not all sleep, but we shall be changed—in a moment, in a twinkling of an eye, at the last trumpet. For the trumpet will sound, and the dead will be raised incorruptible, and we shall be changed."

This is in loving memory of Uncle Larry Baker.

Don't Go So Fast

Slow Down, Slow Down
For you need to stop passing Me by
The road you are traveling
Will quickly cause you to die

You are just a child
Out of your mother's womb
Do not end up before your time
In a graveyard tomb.

Those that I have placed in authority over you
You fail to obey
They are to lead you to the right road
But you are the one choosing to go astray

Allow Me to heal the hurts
And all the brokenness you feel
If you would allow Me
I would come in and your spirit I could heal.

You feel as though no one cares
And no one truly understands
But yet I am here for you
Just take hold of My hand.

I promise I will never leave you
Just draw closer to Me
That we may get to know each other
And you will become who I created you to be.

You do not have to follow the way of death
It is just the enemy
Let the ways of the world go
That every hindering devil may flee.

While you were yet in your mother's womb
I knew you and I ordained you to have a good life
Not to walk around with hate, envy, bitterness, and strife.

I have equipped you to live save
You've been given the ability
For you My only begotten Son I gave
That you may live eternally.

Let go of your old ways
All of that as of **now** must cease
For I love you dearly, my love
And I want you to receive my everlasting Peace!

Don't Go So Fast (enlightened)

Living in the fast lane at an early age can bring about unnecessary trials that could have been avoided. Life is too short, so savor the time. There are small graves all over the world, and some of you know that if it had not been for the Lord's grace and mercy, you would have had your name on a tombstone a long time ago. God cares about all of us, young and old alike. You, as young people, have a special place in the heart of God. Adolescence is not as bad as you make it out to be. Your guardians have been there and done that, and all they want is for you not to make the same mistakes that they made. That is why they are always giving those lectures. Take time to listen and respect the authority that God has placed over your life. Your life depends on it.

Ephesians 6:1-3: "Children obey your parents in the Lord for this is right. Honor thy father and thy mother; which is the first commandment with promise; that it may be well with thee and thou mayest live long on the earth."

Easier Is Not Always Better

Everybody wants
The easy way out
For when trials come
We sometimes begin to doubt

And oftentimes
We tend to lose hope
And declare to the Lord
How we cannot cope

For it's easier to say
We do not care
Than to stand flat-footed
And our cross we bear

It's easier to just walk away
Than to supplicate in prayer for more than a day

How often have we said
Life is not worth the living
And we just give up
Instead of crying out to Jesus
And asking Him to fill our cups

How easy it is to go through life
And just fake it
Than to labor and fight through prayer
And declare you'll make it

To know you're saved
Yet participate in a gossip session
It's not so easy to stand for Christ
And be a model lesson

For this flesh of ours
Will never be saved and it wants to rule
But I dare not end up being
My flesh's fool

For I can't allow my flesh
To bank what my soul can't cash in hell
Therefore I rise in the spirit
For my gifts aren't for sale

Though it maybe rougher than the easy road; be determined
to stand
For I know you can make it with My Father's hand

I encourage you today
From the depths of my heart
God has given you all that you need
So don't sell yourself short

Do not listen to the devil saying
Just sin one more time for the Lord knows your heart
And when judgment day comes you hear the words
Workers of iniquity from my presence depart

Come hell or high water
You need to take heed
Line up with the Word of God
Not just in lip service but also in deeds

Understand, hell was not created for you
So bypass all the enemy's schemes
For your salvation to the devil
Is his worst and evil dream

Easier is not always better
Keep that in mind
For you shall receive a crown of life
If you stand the test of time.

Easier Is Not Always Better (enlightened)

No matter what you go through, there is never a lesson learned if everything is laid out and given to you. If you do not work hard to accomplish things in life, you will never learn the true value from that particular experience. Hard times are not always from the enemy. God needs some soldiers in His army that can stand in the midst of a storm. He cannot get the best use out of you if you've never been proven. You cannot give up every time a hard time comes your way. You cannot follow every doctrine that is appealing to the ear. You cannot allow the enemy to make you feel as though you are in the position of misfortune because you have done this terrible thing to make God angry with you. God has prepared for all of us tailor-made storms, but we need to trust Him in knowing that our storms will not conquer us for He is our overseer. Sometimes you will find yourself in hard places not because of what you have done wrong but for what you have done right. It may look as though the wicked have it easier than those who try to live by the Word, but we cannot go by the way it looks. You must apply your faith and know that God is a God of deliverance and when your time comes He will bring you out. Keep the faith and stop looking for easy street. Travel the road of heartache and the avenue of brokenness, and in the end, you shall find that the roadmap of Jesus, in spite of a few bumps and bruises, will lead you to the road of Victory!

2nd Timothy 2:3: Endure hardships as a good soldier of Jesus Christ.

Fathers, an Awesome Role!

What is the blueprint of man
How did he come to be
This strong authoritative being
Created with such destiny!

Any given male figure of age
Can produce a child
But will the child that comes forth
Be one that is defiled!

Defiled by what
Is the question you may ask
By the rearing of their lives
Of which is an awesome task!

It takes more than just a minute deposit
To have someone call you Dad
In which there has been numerous cases
And that in the eyesight of God is truly sad.

Every father in this world that is willing to believe
Has, by faith, been given what it takes to be a model
role
You just have to be willing to accept Jesus as Lord
And simply ask the Father for strength to purify your
soul.

A father is one
who comes with a price
Their lives are willingly submitted to God
As an ultimate sacrifice!

A father is one
Who has been anointed from on high
For he imitates his Maker
Being that every need of his family he should ultimately
supply!

He is a man of worship, instilling Godly wisdom in his
family
And also the forefront of high praise
The standard in his children
On a daily basis he will raise!

He is the seed-giver of life
A true believer of the Word
Humble, full of humility, and not at all defiant
For a father is the slayer of life's biggest giants!

He is the authority figure
A man of great worth
One who is not afraid
To go on the devil's turf!

A being in creation
As to where God stepped back to say, "Behold, cast
your eyes, and see
I myself have made these men in the very image of
Me!"

Does the message in this poem
Reflect who you are; only you would know
For God entrusted you
To train your children in the way they should go.

After all your children are a reflection of who you are
Whether good or bad, what you plant in them shall
show
I just pray we all get the concept
That we shall reap in our children just what we sow.

To every God-fearing father
I would love to say
I pray for your strength in the Almighty God
And have a wonderful Father's Day!

Fathers, an Awesome Role (enlightened)

Though I do not have practical experience as a father, I do know how my heavenly Father treats me. Therefore I can make this statement to all males – being a sperm donor does not make you a Father. The meaning of a true Father encompasses taking charge of the responsibility of providing necessities for the entire family. It also means providing biblical instructions to your household that you may protect them from the natural as well as the spiritual. A Father protects and provides. A Father is there to provide discipline when necessary and also to shower with love. There is nothing feminine about caring for and loving your child/children. It is your soul responsibility.

Ephesians 6:4: "And, ye **Fathers**, provoke not your children to wrath but bring them up in the nurture and admonition of the Lord."

I dedicate this poem to the love of my life, Minister Ronald L. Benton, who has always given his all to be the best Father any two boys could ever ask for in a lifetime. Thanks, Ronald, for being a true Father.

Feed My Sheep

For I hear the Lord saying:
Touch not my anointing
And do my prophet no harm
For in the spirit
I can hear a frightening alarm
If God has placed upon you
A specific task to do
Know that He is right there with you
Willing to walk you through
We do denounce the works of the enemy
Trying to capture you in fear
That you may not go and do the commandment
God has whispered in your ear
He hears you
In your not-so-sure state
But you know the true answer
For the Lord makes no mistakes
Down a path you have never been before
That you must destroy fallow ground
And plant new seeds
Therefore tune your ear in to Him
And just follow His lead
In a way it is good
That you don't want to go
For then you must really trust Me
And after my Spirit you shall flow
With the words that I give
You shall speak unto men
And no, this will not cause you to make new friends
Yet and still you have all that you need

For I am with you, my child
More than a friend indeed
Put your trust in Me
All of it, I must say
For you trust Me as long as I
Take you the familiar way
I have set you apart
To be used for my glory
That you may cry out aloud
To tell the wonderful story
Of how you once were a twisted mess
But yet I washed you in My Word
That you may now boldly confess
Confess of my goodness
Confess of my grace
Confess how I equipped you
To stay in the race
I ask you, "Do you love Me?"
You say, "Yes, Lord, you know I do"
Then for Me, go with a heart pure and true
I ask again, "Do you love Me?"
"Yes, Lord, my feelings for you are deep"
Then go, my child, go forth and feed my sheep
Stop allowing the enemy to come
Planting unfruitful seeds
He knows deliverance for my people is within you
No, he doesn't want you to do this deed
I understand your feelings
But that will not do
You must know that your feelings
Are not always true
My anointing is with you
Under my wings shall you hide

I only need you to be a willing vessel
And allow me to guide
Stop trying to figure Me out
Just do as I say
That is launch out into the deep
_____, my love
<small>Your name goes here</small>
Go forth and feed my sheep!

Feed My Sheep (enlightened)

God never saves anyone just to save them. If you are a born-again believer and you know that if it had not been for God being on your side that you would have been destroyed long before now, then you need to go forth and be a witness to others that they may be saved, set free from the shackles of the enemy and delivered from the bondages of satan. There are people in this world who are waiting on you to come and minister to them so that they might get what they need from God. No, the preacher cannot do it all. No, the missionaries and the evangelists cannot reach the entire world. We are all supposed to be evangelizing the Word of God. Carry your testimony to the people that you come in contact with on a daily basis so that a door may be opened and you may witness to specific areas in their lives. How many people are going around starving for the Word of God because you have not opened your mouth to feed it to them? We all have someone that God has enabled us to touch and snatch from the enemy. We need to ask God for directions, and when He speaks, we need to move. There is life in the Word of God, and you need to open your mouth and allow the Words that He placed into your spirit to be released, allowing someone else to live! Go forth and feed God's people!

Matthew 9:37: "Then He said to His disciples, The harvest truly is plentiful, but the laborers are few."

Forgiving God

Bless the Lord in all His splendor
Everyone has something to thank Him for
God has been gracious
God has been kind
No other friend like Him on earth will you find
He is faithful and not slack at all
But sometimes flesh gets the best and we
slip and fall
Yet He is there ready and willing
With His arms stretched open wide
And covers us in his protection
And under His wings once again we abide.

Forgiving God (enlightened)

We have all at some point in our Christian lives missed the mark of God. There are some who have missed the mark more than others. It does not matter how many times you have fallen short; the most important thing is that you do not waddle in the mess and feel as though God's grace and mercy can no longer shelter you. God is a God of unconditional love, and there is nothing that you have done that His love cannot cover. If God does not condemn you, do not let anyone else condemn you either. He understands that we, as His children in a non-willing and inhabitual state, will fall short of the calling as to where He has ordained us to walk. All He wants is for you to repent, change your mind (which will result in a change of actions), and keep living for the one who called you, Jehovah God!

Romans 3:23: "For all have sinned and come short of the glory of God."

Get Ready to Go Free

Set your mind
Set your heart
For a word in your spirit
God is getting ready to depart

He knows of your struggles
He knows of your pain
He knows how the enemy
Is trying to bind you in chains

He cares about your future
He knows about your past
He's equipping the saints with faith
That shall move mountains fast

He's getting ready to stir up the gift
That He has placed inside of you
That the words you decree
Shall shake your foundation and make the devil flee

God shall place specific words in your heart
That you shall speak
And by your declaration and faith
You shall put an end to defeat

So strengthen your heart
And be encouraged this day
For the beginning of your miracles
Is only a declaration away

Stir up the gift
That God has given unto you
So you may live in abundance
In which from the beginning he predestined for you to do

God sees your heaviness and your struggles too
Go free, my daughter, go free, my son, for I have already
paid for your liberty
And a deliverance word he has already spoken over you

No need to stay in bondage
I did not die in vain
Nor did I die to have my children go insane

I am a keeper of my word
All you have to do is receive
No longer shall you allow the enemy
To walk around and deceive

Deceive you out of your blessings
And hold back your joy and peace
For I have already spoken to your storms
And I have decreed to them all to cease

By faith receive my word
Put your trust in me
Seize this God-given opportunity
That your spirit may go free.

Get Ready to Go Free (enlightened)

Aren't you tired of living beneath your means? Are you ready to experience the supernatural move of God? I mean wiping debts out and getting titles to possessions that you have not paid for in full. It may sound far-fetched, but that is only because you do not understand what God wants to do for His people. We, as children of God, do not have to stay in bondage in the natural nor the spiritual. Jesus died to set us free from the curse of the law. Everything that exists belongs to God. All we have to do is walk by His principles and watch Him move supernaturally in our lives. If you need a financial blessing pay your tithes and your offering and then give your way out of debt. Sow a seed that shall surely return you a good harvest. If you need a healing, pray for someone else who is sick. Do you want your family members saved? Go out and witness to others who are lost. God wants to free up the church so that others will want what we have. Therefore, if He just has to have someone to represent Him, testify to others and also be a living witness to the supernatural things of God, He just as well use You! Begin to think like God and imitate Him so that you can call forth some things that are overdue in your life.

Deuteronomy 14:28-29: "At the end of every third year you shall bring out the tithe of your produce of that year and store it up within your gates. And the Levite, because he has no portion nor inheritance with you, and the stranger and the fatherless and the widow who are within your gates, may come and eat and be satisfied, that the Lord your God may bless you in all the work of your hand which you do."

God Is Still Worthy

Sometimes life can be hard and misunderstood and things
just don't go our way
But My God is good and we should praise Him in spite of
obstacles throughout our day therefore:

Though my deliverance did not come as I sought for it too
Yet and still thou art God and I will forever praise you

Though my healing did not come at the time I wanted it too
Yet and still thou art God and I will forever adore you

Though my blessing did not come the way I prayed for it
too
Yet and still thou art God and I will forever exalt you

For who should know the mind of God
To dictate to Him what He should do
The trials we face are to bring spiritual insight
In the midst of it all our spirit man is made anew

Because you are God and you know what is best for me
Therefore I surrender my will over to thee

For if I had to deliver myself
I would be a total mess
For without your awesome power
I am truly useless

For you have placed me in this position of life
For such a time as this

And I profoundly hear the Holy Spirit saying,
"Do not rebel"

Lord I pray thy strength to endure
For after this I am sure I will have a burning testimony to
tell

Help me to see that the storms of life that blow my way
Are tailored made to teach me to die to my flesh day by day

I do magnify you Oh Lord
even though I may not understand it all
Yet I am willing to be perfected in You
That I may fulfill my heavenly call

So my encouragement to all that are going through at this
time
Get your eyes off the storm
For Jesus is the Master of the sea
In your designated hour He will deliver thee

For unto that, that He speaks
It has to obey
Just keep your eyes on the prize
For this could very well be your deliverance day!

God Is Still Worthy (enlightened)

I've read in the Bible that one day to God is as a thousand years and a thousand years is as one day. I can hear some in the spirit saying, "Lord, how much longer must I go through this situation? Lord, when will you answer my prayer? I have been in this predicament long enough, and I am ready to come out. I do not believe I can take this much longer." Who are we to tell the Lord when our time has come? He is the one in ultimate control, and if He has you in a place where you do not understand what is going to happen next, maybe He is just trying to get you to trust Him and to walk by faith. If God has brought you to this place in life, He will also bring you through it. He is not a God that abandons His people. Your blessing or your deliverance may not come when or even how you pray for it to, but you have to believe that God is yet working in your favor, because if He wasn't, you know you would have been destroyed by the enemy by now. You are still here because God is working it out. He is still worthy of praise, honor, and glory from your heart no matter what is going on in your life. Praise confuses the enemy!

Philippians 4:12-13: "I know how to be abased, and I know how to abound. Everywhere and in all things I have learned both to be full and to be hungry, both to abound and to suffer need. I can do all things through Christ who strengthens me."

God Knows What You Are Going Through

Do you have problems…
And you feel as though
You have nowhere to turn
Let not your heart be troubled
This you must learn

Believe in the Lord
Have faith not fear
And my Jesus will surely
Wash away your tears

When no one else
Seems to understand and the problems flow
Take it to Jesus
For He already knows

He is great, so very awesome
And I worship Him
He makes the light shine bright
When this world seems dim.

God Knows What You Are Going Through (enlightened)

Do you think there is anything that has ever happened to you that God did not know was going to take place? Let me encourage you today. There will be some things that will happen in our lives that may cause us to say, "If God knew this was going to happen, why didn't He tell me?" Or, some of us may say, "I don't even believe God saw this coming." I want you to know that everything you have been through and every trial that you must yet go through God has already seen the end to it. God has promised us an expected end with a sure future. We sometimes get caught up in the adversities of life and forget about the "Giver" of this life who is Christ. Not only does He know about this thing that looks as if it is going to overtake you, but He also knows how to strategically bring you through it. Never underestimate the immaculate mind of God. He is an untouchable, ever-knowing, mind-boggling God! You may see it in the natural mind one way, but God is spiritual, and the way you see it is far from the way God allows you to go. So whatever situation you find yourself in, just know that God again wants to blow your mind!

Isaiah 55:8-9: "'For My thoughts are not your thoughts, nor are your ways My ways,' says the Lord. 'For as the heavens are higher than the earth, so are My ways higher than your ways, and My thoughts than your thoughts.'"

God Says Live!

A safe place to be
Is in the arms of my God
He is Lord, Savior, My Redeemer
The God Who Is, Who Was, and Is To Come
Bow down, oh spirit-man, and submit unto the only
one who can bring fullness of life to you
He lives, God lives, He is alive and well
Worship Him all ye people of confusion
He will bring peace to your weary souls
Cry, cry, wail out, you men and women of God
His ears are not too heavy that He cannot hear
Nor His arms shortened that He cannot reach
your situation
He sits and waits until He hears a familiar sound—that
is His Word being declared unto Him
Will you sit here forever in this same dry place
and die? God says Live!
Live, even though your marriage is in trouble God
says Live, even though you don't know how you
are going to pay your bills; God says Live even though
you are lonely; God says Live even though you feel
condemned by that sin you just committed; God says
Live, even though your husband/wife is not saved
God says Live even though you are barren and have
not brought forth a child God says Live, even though
you continue to fall short of God's Word repent, be
restored and Live

God says Live, even though your back seems to be pushed against the wall; God says Live! You are not too far away that He cannot reach you! He is just one prayer away from that abundant life.

God Says "Live" (enlightened)

Why do we allow the enemy to come in and kill our hopes and our dreams? Why not stand up to him in spiritual warfare and demand that he loose his hold on everything that belongs to us? Why give in to the ungodly ways? Why not stand for holiness? We all get tired in the flesh but if we could push past our emotions and our feelings and begin to make war in the heavens where satan comes against us we could begin to defeat him and things would begin to align with the word of God. The only thing we need to allow to die is our flesh-our way of doing things. Anything beyond that whether it be dead marriages, dead finances, dead worship, dead faith or even dead hopes and dreams I believe they have died prematurely and you need to petition God who is the giver of life to revive you situation and declare it to live again. Today, I challenge you to go back and unwrap by faith everything you gave up on and begin to revive it by speaking the word of God over every dead area in your life.

John 11:25: "I am the resurrection and the life. He who believes in Me, though he may die, he shall live."

God's Authority

My people, saith the Lord of Host
Put on thy strength
There is more that I have to offer you being that the
veil has been rent
Fresh anointing if you would just stay in my will
Great victories have I predestined you to fulfill
Enter with me into the holies of holy
That I might whisper in your ear
What I would permit you to declare boldly
Without doubt or fear
That I Am that I Am; The Beginning and the End;
A well of Living Water
I will cause you to never thirst again
Oh magnify Me for I am worthy to be praised
For I am the only one who causes the dead to be
raised
It is I who causes blind eyes to see
Not to mention at the Name of Jesus
Every devil must flee
Never underestimate My authority
For I myself parted the Red Sea
Moses held the staff but he really held Me.
Now what is it that you need Me to be?
I am the way, the truth, and the life
You do not have to live in fear, torment, and strife
I have already defeated Satan who walks around as a
roaring lion
Therefore have confidence in Me and stop your
fruitless whining

For greater is he that is in you than he that is in the world
For you are My chosen people
More precious than diamonds or pearls
I am the Highest God
The Prince of Peace and I have come to give you rest, even now
My daughter, My son
Just get ready for the best
My Word is true and I am God, I cannot lie
Therefore if you hold to my vision
You can kiss your troubles good-bye
For even your biggest dilemma is under my authority
And I now command all the chains in your life to loose their hold
And I declare you to go free!

God's Authority (enlightened)

The authority of God is not to be compared to that of a mere man. God is Sovereign—the supreme ruler of all mankind. Every word that is spoken from of the mouth of God has already been approved by Him. So why are you waiting on someone to validate the Word that God has spoken over your life? That which comes from the mouth of God shall be manifested, within your life, in the fullness of time.

Numbers 23:19: "God is not a man that He should lie; neither the Son of man that He should repent: hath He said, and shall He not do it? Or hath He spoken, and shall He not make it good?"

God's Unfailing Love

Because of your goodness
Because of your grace
Because you helped me
To stay in the race.

Those times I should have fallen
Those times I should have failed
Those very times that I should have been destined for
hell.
It was those times you were there to pick me up and
help me to travail.

Lord, your mercy is everlasting
Why do you care so much for me?
You rescued me in the day of tribulation
And in the day of adversity.

You come with thou anointing
You come with your grace
To shower me with love
To pour into my faith.

The tears that I've cried
You wiped from my eyes
You gave to me for my ashes of mourning
The oil of gladness in the dawning.

Now I rejoice in your goodness
I rejoice in your love
For showering me with blessings
That you sent from up above.

I truly, My God, say thank you
For loving me as you do
I give to you my whole life
As a sacrafice from me to you.

Do with it as you please
For my life is not my own
I surrender my will over unto you
That you may receive glory upon your throne.

Yes, Lord Jesus
I am yours forevermore
Shape me, Lord, and mold me, God
That I may hear "well done" as I enter heaven's door.

God's Unfailing Love (enlightened)

Have you ever asked the question, "God, as much as I have fallen short and as much as I still fail you, why do you continue loving me?" If you are like me, you should have been consumed a long time ago. Surely we have failed enough within this lifetime for God to wash his hands of us and to count us as doomed. But His love and His mercy endures forever. It does not matter how much you think you should have been counted out, nor does it matter how much the devil tries to trip you up, God always speaks a word and equips you again for life's challenges. You will never master all that life has to throw your way, but just know that God is the master of life and love!

Jeremiah 31:3-4: "The Lord has appeared of old to me saying: Yes, I have loved you with an everlasting love; Therefore with loving kindness I have drawn you. Again I will build you, and you shall be rebuilt."

Harden Not Your Hearts

Harden not your hearts
For what others to you have done
Just think back to how
We crucified the Son
Yet he held not a grudge
Against you nor me
But instead he prayed
"Father, let them be."

Harden not your hearts
Against those that curse you
In a big way or small
We cannot afford to hold unforgiveness
In our hearts at all
For if it had not been for some of your enemies
You would have never stopped your evil deeds

Harden not you hearts
Against those that devise wickedness against you
For if you think back far enough
I'm sure you've acted wickedly to more than a few

Can you abide by the Word
Do good to those by whom you're hated and despised
Can you see your enemy from your Father's eyes
Or can you see only the bad they've done to you
As if you've never sown discord, too
The testimony really is not for them
But it's for you
For if God can deliver thou
Surely he can deliver them, too

Pray for those by whom you are persecuted
And also mistreated
For then you are doing the works of Christ
And this guarantees that the devil is defeated

If you love them who love you
What are you doing to show Christ's example
For he placed you in the kingdom
To be a model sample
Of just who he really is
For he has dressed you in himself, therefore you are
anointed
Now, as an ambassador of Christ, are you walking in
that in which you were appointed

So what do you do more than these
For even sinners love their own
You've been saved all these years
So let the love of Christ be shown

Guard your heart in all things
For out of it flow the issues of life
We have no time for the devil's games
Walking around in bitterness and strife

Glorify God
Not only in words
But also in deeds
To these words hearken and take heed.

Harden Not Your Hearts (enlightened)

What is the true purpose of our enemies—whether it be the enemy in the natural world or the enemy in the spiritual realm? Why did God place them in our lives to continue to distract us and to try to get us off course with God? The fact of the matter is our enemies were created not to harm us but to help push us in the direction of God. If it had not been for some of our enemies, we would not have taken the time to pray, praise, or worship. God puts certain obstacles in our lives to keep us humble and to knock us to our knees in prayer. He knows what we are capable of; therefore, we need to tell the Lord "thank you" because if it were not for our enemies, we would not have made it to that next level in God. Do not allow your flesh to get involved in what God is doing in you. So, the next time you feel overwhelmed and weighed down, just remember God is in ultimate control.

2 Timothy 2:3-4: "You therefore must endure hardship as a good soldier of Jesus Christ. No one engaged himself with the affairs of this life, that he may please him who enlisted him as a soldier."

Highway to Heaven

I was riding down a road, a road of distress
Seemed like life's heavy burdens never let me rest
I started out on the corner of East Sin St.
I rode for years head-on with defeat
I rode until my gas needle fell on **Grace**
I finally realized my spirit-man hadn't been embraced
I realized I was driving but sleeping behind the wheel
Satan was on the loose; It was out to kill
I saw an exit that read **Conviction Highway** two miles straight
I had to go before it was too late
I saw my life from the outside looking in—full of agony, full of sin
I got back on the road only to see straight up ahead the blessed street of **Mercy**
And there were angels saying, come in, my child come in and let my Father give you rest
For it is my Father that knows your situation best
He said, "Stay on this road and you shall stand, Put your hand in the Master's hand"
Oh yes, I did obey this command and now I'm in the Master's plan
I rode on and I rode on fast to approach nothing more than the **Holy Ghost** bypass
As He was abiding in me as we were joining, He led me directly to the street of **Anointing.**

Highway to Heaven (enlightened)

We all start out in one common state: sinful. We all have an opportunity at some point in life to make a conscious decision to choose either the road of life that will fulfill our destiny to God or the road that will make our bed in hell. The choice is completely up to you. You do not have a disadvantage just because you grew up in "the hood." You should not look at accepting Christ with a negative aspect because you were raised in a single-parent home. You do not have a disadvantage just because you had a hard life growing up. In fact, these things work for your good. God made us all who we are and what we are, and he made all of us beautiful. You may not have mattered to anybody else, but you matter to God. What better person to be used by God than the transformed prostitute on the corner or the recovered wino from the back alley. You have the power and the ability to be used by God if only you surrender your life over to Him. God is not going to accept any lame excuses on Judgment Day for why you did not choose the road of life. Choose life today and follow Christ. He allows U-turns!

Deuteronomy 30:15-16: "See, I have set before you today life and good, death and evil, in that I command you today to love your God, to walk in his ways, and to keep His commandments, His statutes, and His judgments, that you may live and multiply; and the Lord your God will bless you in the land which you go to possess."

I Am God

Be still and know that I am God!
Be still and know that I am God!
My lovely, my righteousness, come to Me and don't distress
For I'm, I'm God, I am God!

Be still and know that I am God!
Rest in me—Rest in me
I am here, here with thee
Be still and know that I am God!

I hold the world in my hands; I hold thy pain
There will be sunshine after the rain
For I am, I am, I am God!

Be still, Be still
Oh weary soul
Be still, Be still
And let thy eyes behold

My majesty, my glory
My awesomeness, my righteousness,
Behold thy peace, behold my joy
I am here today forevermore.
Be still, Be still
For I am GOD!

I Am God (enlightened)

Why are you so anxious? Why do you fear the future? What thrill do you get out of worrying? Why do you sit up at night unable to sleep, toiling over tomorrow and dealing with the stress of today? Don't you want to enter into the rest and the peace of God? God never meant for His people to be tormented by life. Allow God to settle your spirit that you may walk in true peace and prosperity. Stop trying to play "god" in your situation. Just let God be God! Turn over to Him every situation in your life that is out of control and watch Him work it out for your good. Allow God to turn your mess into a testimonial message! Once you surrender your all to God, He is obligated to come and be a defender of the righteous.

Psalms 46:10: "Be still, and know that I am God; I will be exalted among the nations, I will be exalted in the earth!"

I'm Coming

Off of my throne
I'm getting ready to stand
I shall rise
I'm coming to get those who
Through me have been justified

I am coming soon
With all glory, power, and majesty
I will remove all saints
To rise and be with Me eternally.

Now you sinner-man
Where will thou goest
Only to the den of hell
To be tormented in the degree of the lowest

You shall inherit fire and brimstone
And the gnashing of teeth
Only for the very reason
You forever denied Me.

Listen to that old trickster, the very enemy
Trying to talk to you saying this is just a rhyme
Don't take heed to those words
For you have plenty of time

He is a liar
And a deceiver, too
If you die today and go to hell
He will still be laughing at you.

Rise above in your spirit
Rise up every woman and every man
Put your life in the Master's hand
That you may be a part of his will and plan.

He said, come unto me
All that are burdened and are heavily laden
And I will give you rest
Don't listen to the enemy that tries to make you settle
for less

Your life has value
God has prepared heaven, not hell, to be your home
Will you choose the streets of gold
Or will you stay with fire and brimstone?

The choice is yours
God gave us a free will
Will you now give your life to Christ
That your true purpose would be fulfilled?

I'm Coming (enlightened)

The Lord's coming is not far off. It is closer than we realize. Your soul will have to give an account of every evil deed that has been done in your flesh. You may say you do not lie, cheat, steal, curse, or drink. You may say, "I treat everybody right, and I do not do this or I do not do that." Let me enlighten you – being morally good is not going to get you into heaven. Confessing Christ and surrendering your life to Him is the only sure way to gain eternal life. Why not make the choice today? What do you have to lose except a ticket to hell?

Matthew 24:44: "Therefore you also be ready, for the Son of Man is coming at an hour you do not expect."

Lord, You Know

Lord, only you know; Lord, only you know
I say I will; I say I'll go
But, Lord, only you know.

My heart is willing
And I want to do thy will
But when the time comes
My purpose I don't fulfill
I say I will; I say I'll go
But, Lord, only you know; Only you know

Anoint me, Lord, put thy gift in me
I will then use it to the best of my God-given ability
That's what we pray
But when the time comes, we run the other way
I say I will, My heart says yes, I say I'll go
But, Lord, only you know; Only you know.

Make it plain, Lord
For me to hear that I may obey when You speak
And when You do, my spirit dies down
Also my faith grows weak.
I say I will, I say I'll go
But, Lord, only You know; Only You know.

I really want to do thy will
And give it my all, my very best
But it seems as though
I'm always failing the test.

But yet I want to do thy will
My heart really says "yes"
And thy will, in it I would love to flow
Lord, You know; Oh Lord, only You know.

Take not your hand away from my life
Rid me of all envy and strife
Obedient is what I am striving to be
Grant me a willing spirit, Lord, to sustain me.

I hear your call, My Lord
I hear it loud and clear
I even hear you saying,
"My child, do not fear"
I want to step out
I really, really do—I want to go
Lord, only you know; Only you know!

I have confidence in you, my God
So being that you do know
I am all yours, my God
Hold my hand and I will go!

Lord, You Know (enlightened)

In desperate attempts to try to please God, you stand elevated in spirit and you make a courageous statement: "Lord, whatever you want me to do or whatever you want me to achieve for you, Lord, I will do it." You want to take that step of faith and just sell out to the Lord, but it seems as though every time you make up your mind to do what He tells you to do, the enemy raises his ugly head in a desperate attempt to hinder you. When the moment of truth comes, we are like Peter saying, "God who?" Lord, you want me to do what? I just don't believe I am hearing the Lord. We make up all kinds of awkward excuses in trying to justify the reason why we did not obey the voice of the Lord. God understands the heart of man. You were created by Him, and He already knows about all of your struggles. He knows about that issue that tries to confine you and keep you from stepping out. Let me encourage you today. Take the step of faith wholeheartedly, and God will do the rest. He is just waiting on you to launch out into the deep.

Psalms 7:1: "O Lord my God, in you I put my trust."

My Call

Some things you can get others to substitute for your doing

But for what God called you to do, you must get a knowing.

A knowing of who God is and what He is calling you to be.

This is a job **just** for **you**; no, you can't throw it onto me.

Think it not strange the visions you see or the task before you.

God is calling a remnant of people who are faithful and true.

No one else can do your job.

Do you say you are for God's house but keep allowing the saints to be robbed?

For God says you have just what they need.

You endured those rigid trials so that in your belly He may plant those fruitful seeds.

Go forth and do thy will for then and only then will your true purpose be fulfilled.

Go now, you daughters of Zion; go now, you mighty men of valor; do what God has told you to do.

For in obedience to the voice of God there is a blessing awaiting you!

My Call (enlightened)

As Christians, we all have a ministry to fulfill. You may never preach a sermon, but the lives we live preach every day. You may never travel the world to do the work of an evangelist, but you should carry the Word and evangelize to those God allows to cross your path. You may never teach a Bible study lesson, but you should study the Bible to show yourself approved by God. You should always be ready and willing to share the gospel with those that are lost. You have a ministry, and it is significant in the eyes of God. If God called you to hold the door post in church, do it to the best of your ability. If God called you to usher, usher in his people as if you are ushering in God, Himself. If He called you to intercede for others, pray without ceasing and look for your reward from on high. Stop trying to carry out someone else's ministry and stop trying to put your ministry on others. Commit your ministry unto God that you may execute it to His glory.

2 Timothy 4:5: "Be watchful in all things, endure afflictions, do the work of an evangelist, fulfill your ministry."

My Comforter

I did not have knowledge of strength
He blessed me with Power
I went against his will
He forgave me
I sat around all sad and down
He brought me joy
I thought no one cared for me
Love knocked on my heart's door
Everyone mistreated me—even myself
He introduced love
I dibbled all around in sin
He tied holiness to my soul
I was scared, so very afraid
He clothed me with security
I couldn't see my way through life
He molded my eyes into faith
I thought I had no power—useless me
He dressed me with anointing
I thought I was destined for hell
He gave me his life.

My Comforter (enlightened)

Whatever it is that you need God to be, he will be just that for you. Do not sit around and have a pity party with the devil. Stop saying you are not worthy. Stop saying you are defeated. Do not let communication depart from your mouth that does not line up with the Word of God. God sent His Holy Spirit to bring you comfort and so all truth may abide with you. You are more than a conqueror. You are victorious! You are the head and not the tail. You are the lender and not the borrower! See yourself as God sees you and tell the devil he is a liar and you do not accept what he has to offer. Your words frame your very life. Receive God's Word in your heart today.

John 14:16-18: "And I will pray the Father, and He will give you another Helper, that He may abide with you forever—the Spirit of truth, whom the world cannot receive, because it neither sees Him nor knows Him, for He dwells with you and will be in you. I will not leave you orphans; I will come to you."

My Cry

God,
Sometimes I feel so confused
Sometimes I feel ultimately misused
There are other times I feel my words cannot say
All that I really want to express
Why must I continue to battle in my flesh
The enemy truly despises me
And I hate him even more
Lord, help me to raise my standards in You
That I will not leave him an open door.
Sometimes even with all my friends
I feel very sorrowful and lonely within
And I know this void only you can fill
Teach me to submit to your perfect will
There are days that I feel
I try to do everything right
Yet it seems no use
Then I cry out to you and a life-giving word you loose
I am grateful for you, God
For always being there for me
And out of every adverse situation
You always allow me to see
That it is for your glory
That your will for me be done
I truly love you, Lord
I am thankful to your dear Son
Continue to break me, Lord
Purge and cleanse me from myself
And I know when the process is complete
You will be able to use the portion of me that is left.

My Cry (enlightened)

It does matter to God how discouraged and misused you may feel. It also matters to Him when you feel like the weight of the world is on your shoulders. What we must remember is the fact that God is who He says He is. He is our deliverer! He is our burden bearer! He is our refuge! He is our strong tower! It is the enemy's job to bring discouragement and confusion. You do not have to be defeated by him. You are not the only one that is going through a trial. Stand steadfast and do not be moved from your designated place in God. The greater the anointing, the greater the persecutions. Get ready to be established by God in your set place. Let that devil know that he is defeated as he has been from the very beginning; so, therefore, be determined to stay with God. You can weather the storm. It is only a test.

1 Peter 5:8-10: "Be sober, be vigilant; because your adversary the devil walks about like a roaring lion, seeking whom he may devour. Resist him, steadfast in the faith, knowing that the same sufferings are experienced by your brotherhood in the world. But may the God of all grace, who called us to His eternal glory by Christ Jesus, after you have suffered a while, perfect, establish, strengthen, and settle you."

On the Cross

What a fine example
We have to live by
Up on the cross
He didn't even sigh
Free-willed and boldly
Did He obey
The long-suffering for me
I could never repay
The pain He took
Just for me
So I could live eternally
Every strike He took
The feeling absurd
For every feeling of pain
He most likely spoke Word
That precious blood
Dripping down
Yet and still
He wore no frown
I'm in the city
Jesus died to set me free
So I could spend my eternal life
In the kingdom of glory.

On the Cross (enlightened)

When Jesus was on the cross, He willingly went through the will of God for His life. He prayed one prayer in particular and that was, "If it be thy will, let this cup pass from me."
Then He quickly said, "Not my will, but thy will be done." Whose will do you want done in your life? We always find something to murmur and complain about. Why is it when we find ourselves in one of life's storms we get a mouthful of "woe is me"? Don't you know your winds of life push you to your next level in God? You were not put here to have everything put on a silver platter for you. Those with the true anointing of God have been crushed in spirit and torn in emotions, yet they know how to bless their God. Never lose your praise! Jesus always led by example. Who or what is leading you?

Matthew 16:24: "Then Jesus said to His disciples, If anyone desires to come after Me, Let him deny himself and take up his cross and follow me."

Packing Power

Because I serve the living God
I can serve notice to the enemy
If you serve Him also
You, too, have the power to make the devil flee
Yet it has absolutely nothing to do with you
This power comes from on high
You can't do it on your own
So there's no need to try
For it has nothing to do with who I am
But everything to do with whose I am
The child of the sacrificial Lamb
I am the possession
Of the Almighty God-Jesus
That man that hung upon a tree
Has given me the authority
To charge every demonic force to flee
This packing-power authority
Does not come easily
I had to release my will over to the Lord
That I could flow in my
God-given authority
I had to purify my life
And live holy every day
Not just when I wanted
Things to go my way
Giving up those things
That my flesh loved so much
To be placed on the potter's wheel
For this divine potter's touch
Day by day I laid aside weights

That set me off course
That my ears may be trained
To hear God's voice
Yet it was a yielding of my inner man
Completely my choice
The reward of my obedience caused me to
Operate in the Holy Ghost with force
Denying myself frequently
That my flesh may decrease
My spirit-man getting stronger
Every tactic of the enemy
He empowered me to cease
Did this happen overnight
I tell you, "NO!"
Yet the more you
Consecrate yourself to God
Higher in the spirit you shall go
Packing this power comes with a price
The more power you pack
The greater your sacrifice
Does God only have certain ones
That this authority belongs to?
Certainly not, for if you die to your will,
sell out to God completely, you can pack power, too.

Packing Power (enlightened)

Do not be like the seven sons of Sceva, trying to walk on territory you've never experienced. Stop trying to pray like everybody else; stop trying to speak in those stolen tongues. With every level of tongues comes a higher level of demons. As far as you know, the one you are trying to imitate may be imitating someone else. Pursue Jesus. Imitate your maker. Be a duplicate of Christ. If you really want to pack power, be honest with yourself and God. Be led by the Spirit. Get to know God for yourself and experience Him like never before.

2 Corinthians 4:7: "But we have this treasure in earthen vessels, that the excellence of the power may be of God and not of us."

Pastor

Pleasing in the sight of God. A great
Asset to the kingdom. You are always
Seeking to serve others with a spirit
Tailor-made by His Word. Remember God has
Ordered your steps and He sees you as
Righteous before His people.

Pastor (enlightened)

I truly extend heartfelt gratitude to my pastor (Charles Lewis) and co-pastor (Lisa Lewis) of Antioch United Holy Church. In more ways than one, you both challenge the body of believers to elevate their faith in God and to never give up. Thank you both for submitting yourselves to God that he may pour into your spirit and, in turn, you pour into mine. It is because of your prayers and dedication to Christ, I, through your ministry, have become transformed into the newness of life! Continue to allow God to use you in such an awesome way. It is from your mouths that I receive the bread of life that allows me to continue to live in the midst of trials and tribulations. I love you both from the heart.

Jeremiah 23:4: "'I will set up shepherds over them who will feed them; and they shall fear no more, nor be dismayed, nor shall they be lacking,' says the Lord."

Patience

Patience is the key
To a great deal of things
It is the key especially
To the blessings God brings

Even though you ask today
And you don't receive tomorrow
Believe in God
He shall wash away all your sorrows

You must ask
And be a firm believer
You must be
An open receiver

You must learn to be patient
And wait on the Lord
And if you travel with Him
The burden won't be so hard.

Patience (enlightened)

Be careful what you pray for. Praying for patience opens a door for trying encounters with friends and enemies. God already knows how you will handle each circumstance, yet He wants you to know exactly what you still need to work on in your life. We must all go through trials and tribulations. As we go through life's storms, we must remember that we have the Master of the Sea on board. We then need to rest in knowing that Jesus has our best interests at heart no matter what the situation. Stop complaining and do not gripe another day. Stop crying; go on and dry your tears. Jesus is only molding you into a more powerful creation. Use the principles that He has given us for each given situation. Apply your faith to the situation, for that is the only thing that moves God.

James 1:3: "My brethren, count it all joy when you fall into various trials, knowing that the testing of your faith produces patience. But let patience have its perfect work, that you may be perfect and complete, lacking nothing."

Peacemaker

He gave me love
When I thought no one cared
He gave me peace
When I thought I couldn't bear
The problems of life
That seemed so real
But when I met Jesus
He said, "Peace, be still!"

Peacemaker (enlightened)

A chaotic state we sometimes find ourselves in. We know that we are doing the things that are biblically required of us, but yet it seems as though the more we press into God, the more our lives become disordered. You don't even know why you are still standing. You know you should have lost your mind by now or even your very life, yet God is a good God and He allows peace to flood your soul in the midst of adverse situations. Understand that the greatest disturbance in a storm comes right before a great calm. What I am saying is that if you are going through a storm and you know that things cannot get any worse, get ready for your miracle. It is on the way! Hold fast to your faith. You've made it this far, and there is no reason to give up now. Make the devil out to be the liar that he is! I believe by faith that Jesus is speaking to your situation right now, and it has to obey the voice of God!

James 4:6-7: "Be anxious for nothing, but in everything by prayer and supplication, with thanksgiving, let your request be known unto God; and the peace of God, which surpasses all understanding, will guard your hearts and minds through Christ Jesus."

Plant on Good Ground

Today is the day
We plant our seed
To fall on good ground
Not to grow up as a weed
For some seeds sown
Are unholy and men they try to bound
Yet with surety, goodness, and mercy
God shall cut them down
Even though this pit seed
May be sown and grown
Be very careful for
The seed you plant may be your own.

Plant on Good Ground (enlightened)

What is a seed? It is a small, fertilized cell that is capable of sprouting to produce a new product. We plant seeds all the time. We can have seeds of faith as well as seeds of doubt. Even the words we say are seeds that either bring forth life or death. How can you tell what seeds you are allowing to be cultivated in your life? One way is to examine the fruit in your life. What are you producing? I do not only mean the material things in life, but also the intangible fruit, such as love, joy, peace, long-suffering, kindness, goodness, faithfulness, gentleness, and self-control. These are the seeds that shape and mold your life to be all that God created you to be. Now I ask the question, what are you fertilizing with your mouth? What are you producing on a daily basis?

Proverbs 18:21: "Death and life are in the power of the tongue, And those who love it will eat its fruit."

You Too Can Possess the Keys to the Kingdom!

To possess the keys
You must give up sin
Gossiping, cheating, and backbiting
All these things that are within.

Within your heart
Even after you said you've been freed
The very nature of the devil
Lives and breeds.

How can we walk in our dominion
And call things to come to be
When God sees no difference
In the sinner-man and me

Get rid of that mess
Don't hold it in your heart
Don't permit God to say
Workers of iniquity from my presence depart.

Walk in your inheritance
Jesus **died** and **rose** to make us free
In confusion and bondage
A child of God should not be.

Make up in your mind this day
To do what is right
And watch your spiritual life
Arise to new heights.

You Too Can Possess the Keys to the Kingdom
(enlightened)

God has given us the keys to the kingdom. He has made the way to life obtainable, and we did not even have to die a natural death. His Son paid the price for all of us. All we are commanded to do is to keep His law and His statutes. We do not have to live in sickness, poverty, bondage, lack, or fear! We can enjoy abundant life right here on earth if we would just surrender our wills to God and follow His instructions. Jesus went into the belly of Hades and retrieved the keys of death and hell from the devil. He has given each of us a way of escape, and all we have to do is believe in Him. It is your rightful inheritance. Every door of prosperity that needs to be opened in your life can be if you just accept Jesus as your personal Savior. You, too, can possess the keys to the kingdom.

Deuteronomy 15:4-5: "Except when there may be no poor among you; for the Lord will greatly bless you in the land which the Lord your God is giving you to possess as an inheritance—**only** if you carefully obey the voice of the Lord your God, to observe with care all these commandments which I command you today."

Power Lies in Jesus' Name

P - The <u>P</u>ersonality that the Holy Spirit brings
O - How the <u>O</u>vercomer makes the heavenly
  bells ring
W - The strength you have <u>W</u>ithin
E - The <u>E</u>ternity not spent in hell for sin
R - All the more <u>R</u>eason you have to live for God

Power In His Name (enlightened)

We all want to be anointed. We all want God to demonstrate Himself in our lives by the works that we do for Him. We all want the manifestation of His glory. Who wants to be purified? Who desires to be sanctified? Who pleads to God to allow them to be consecrated and set apart to be a vessel of honor in the ministry? Who desires true integrity? When you begin to walk in the "show nuff" power of God, you gain the very personality of Christ. No more walking around with hate in your heart, "woman of God," and no more sowing discord among the saints, "man of God." If we, as children of God, want to walk in the anointing, we better ask God to purify our hearts and purge us of all unrighteousness. We need to be lovers of God and not of man! By what spirit or power do you operate?

2 Timothy 3:5: "Having a form of godliness but denying the power thereof."

Prayer of Protection

Holy One, Father
I come now to thee
For you are the only one
Who can set me free

Stretch forth thine hand
That the adversary may know
The blood of Jesus is upon me
And he is a defeated foe

Victory is mine
Forever and evermore
For the sins of your people
Up on the cross you bore

Praises be to the Father
And peace be unto you
For this life we all live
Should be set apart and true!

Prayer of Protection (enlightened)

Do you fear God for naught? Do you believe in the prayer of faith that you pray? Can you lay hands upon yourself when you or a loved one becomes ill? Your prayers are powerful. When you stand before God in His righteousness, He does not see you in the natural, but He sees His Son standing before Him because you are covered in His blood. Go boldly before the throne of God and petition Him as never before, because you are powerful in the eyes of God!

James 5:16: "The effective, fervent prayer of a righteous man avails much."

Psalms 23

V1: "The Lord is my shepherd I shall not want."

(I am your overseer. I watch over you. I commissioned you to this call, not man. Stop asking these questions to other people or even in your mind: "Can I really do this?" "Do you really think He called me?" I have already spoken into your spirit so therefore it is! You shall not lack in faith, power, or in the anointing for I have dressed you in My anointing and this clothing you cannot take off. Why have I dressed you and not the next one? Because I chose you and I choose whom I will. You are my chosen one. A part of that anointing is because I laid My hands on you, and you did not have to work for it. There is an anointing that you get by seeking My face and putting off the things of the world. The more you stay in tune and fellowship with Me, the more anointed you shall be.)

V2: "He makes me to lie down in green pastures; He leads me beside the still waters."

(Rest where you are. Though you do not fully realize it, you are already flourished and a great size you shall become. Know that where I send you there will be no confusion.)

V3: "He restores my soul. He leads me in the paths of righteousness for His name's sake."

(I will continue to pour into you as you give out of your spirit. It is not because of you but solely because of Me. You are on the right path for I have My own reputation to uphold, and I do not commission anyone to work in My Name, and I know they are not capable.)

V4: "Yea, though I walk through the valley of the shadow of death, I will fear no evil; for thou art with me. Your rod and Your staff, they comfort me."

(Yes, there are some valleys that you will have to walk through, but you walk in Me. Take your eyes off of the valley and look to the hill from which cometh your help. When you are in the valley, you can see Me better. In your lowest times, I am still there. Take your eyes off of the distractions and put them on the God that made heaven and the earth. Your biggest distraction is under my authority. When you walk among those dead situations that I will cause to come your way and those stagnated people that walk but are dead because they do not have life on the inside of those broken hearts and those of a distraught spirit, fear not for I am with you. I will cause life to spring forth out of you. That life connects with them, and they shall in turn be resurrected and come alive by the authority that I have given unto you. I am with you. I will lead you and guide and comfort you. My Holy Spirit will be as a rod and a staff to you. Listen to His voice on the inside of you and obey His every command.)

V5: "You prepare a table before me in the presence of my enemies; You anoint my head with oil; My cup runs over."

(And as for those who speak in opposition of what I have told you to do, those who say you could never, will never do this in which I have told you to do, and those that say you do not have what it takes—those very ones shall be exposed, even the devil himself, so therefore be careful even how you view yourself for you no longer belong to yourself but to Me! For I am preparing you now even in the midst of your unbelief. Do not be an enemy unto yourself. Yes, I will establish you in this earth that you may witness of Me and cause others to believe. Yes, you will even be established with great riches (overflow). I will make your name great in this earth.)

V6: "Surely goodness and mercy shall follow me all the days of my life and I shall dwell in the house of the Lord Forever."
(Do not doubt, rest assured, be confident and unmovable in the spirit. I make you a promise and it is so that Goodness—stay in Me and ask what you will according to your measure of faith and to My Word, and it shall be fulfilled. To My goodness nothing could be compared, for it shall follow you wherever you go; it is there. Now for Mercy—My protection, My redemption, My Blood, My grace, My favor, shall no doubt follow you for it came from Me and it follows that it knows. My Goodness and My Mercy shall follow you all the days of your life and when your assignment is complete, your mansion on high awaits you! You shall have a house not made by man's hands! Go forth and be of good courage, and I shall strengthen your heart.)

Psalms 23 (enlightened)

To everyone that is serious about the things of God and the things that concern their ministry—whether your ministry is preaching, teaching, or just being a good friend—God is the only one who can make full use of what He has instilled in you. He is right there in the midst of your fear, discouragement, and even your failures. Nothing has ever been perfected without trial and error. Use your gift at all costs to glorify God.

Romans 8:30: "Moreover whom He predestined, these He also called; whom He called, these He also justified, and whom He justified, these He also glorified."

Repent and Go On

I thank you, God
For convicting me
I thank you, Lord
For not letting me be
I thank you for
This uneasy feeling
For I know then
With my spirit you are dealing
For whether it is
What we call a really big sin or just a little white lie
It should not be
For you have commanded
That our flesh must die
Thank you for letting me know
That after the devil's schemes I should not go
I am holy and righteous all because of you
So wash me again, Lord, through and through
Yes, I failed you, but please forgive me, Lord
Yet the last time I know I asked the same
I take this spiritual walk seriously
I realize this is not a game
I do not want to take
Advantage of your grace
So Lord, I surrender my all
Help me, Oh God, to stay in the race
You are such a forgiving God
I love you so
And after your spirit
I choose to flow
Thank you, Father, for forgiving me

And making my heart ever so light
For giving me a spirit of repentance
And spiritual insight
I know that the enemy wants me to quit
Therefore the kingdom of God I would not be fit
But you, Oh Lord, are my saving grace and my strong
tower
I give you praise for my deliverance at this very hour
Be strong, saith the Lord
As far as it is with me
I have already forgotten the sin
And cast it into the forgettable sea
The devil is the one who wants you to continue to trip
over your mess
And to never allow you to see you at your best
Yet I am a God that takes your mess and turns it into a
testimony
For I am drawn to true repentance
And not one that is phony
For if you truly repent from your falls you will turn
away
It's not something you practice each and every day
This is not for those
Called by my Name
Nor for those that seek self-fame
But as for you I will Proclaim
Go in peace and sin no more
For your sins be forgiven you
Let not your heart be sore
You are my child
You are still blessed
Your sins to me and me alone
You have truly confessed

All that I require
Is that your heart remains pure
For then, my love
You can rest assured
That you are walking in peace
As I commanded you before
So do not fret
Over this thing anymore
Remember this one thing
When you go wrong
Repent genuinely
And in your heart I will place a brand new song!

Repent and Go On (enlightened)

Do not use the word repent lightly. Some of us willingly go out and sin and say, "Well, God knows my heart." Yes, He does. He knows if you are putting forth your best effort to try and live by His Word. You may fall short from time to time and whole-heartily repent. Yet, God knows if you are using the word repent as justification to justify your everyday habitual sins and in your heart of hearts you know as well. God is a forgiving God but we must not take advantage of His grace and His mercy. Repentance means to turn away from sin or anything that distracts you from doing the perfect will of God. Simply put, repenting means to change your mind about a particular matter. We all have issues of life that causes us to fall into temptations that the enemy brings before us. Yet, God has already given us a way of escape. No, you can not live in this world and not fall short of God's Word but you can have a heart to serve the Lord sincerely and when those times come that you see you have missed the mark arise, dust yourself off and keep living for God. Do not allow your short-comings to discredit your walk with God. In fact, God is a God that uses your mess ups to be a witness to others. Do not get caught up in the pleasures of sin. Judge yourself then you will not have a need to be judged by another. Once God reveals to you the area(s) that needs to be dealt with allow Him to cleanse, wash and purify your mind, body and soul. Are there some things that you need to change your mind about today?

Revelation 3:3: "Remember therefore how you have received and heard; hold fast and repent. Therefore if you will not watch, I will come upon you as a thief, and you will not know what hour I will come upon you."

Who Is He?

Who loves you
When you are sick
And heals you
Of your aching pains

Who's there for you
When your world seems black
And brings you in
From the storms and rain

Who's love is priceless
Like a bird it is free
Who's love is so very
gracious to thee

Who's always there to listen to your problems
When others are gone
Who's always there for you
And never leaves you alone

Have you figured it out yet
Well, let's see
God, is the only one
I know it to be!

Who Is He (enlightened)

He is our sustainer and the lifter of our heads. He is our way-maker, our strong tower, and our deliverer! He is our peace! He is our grace and our mercy! He Is The Great I Am That I Am! He is our victory and our Lord! He is King of Kings and Lord of Lords! He is our scapegoat! He is our Advocate! He is Eternal! He is All-Powerful! He is All-Knowing; Holy; The Lamb of God; The Resurrection and The Life; Master; Faithful and True Witness; Our Rock; High Priest; The Door; Living Water; Bread of Life; Rose of Sharon; Alpha and Omega; Our Teacher; The Light of The World; The Image of The Invisible God; The Author and The Finisher of Our Faith; The Way, Truth, and The Light; Our Redeemer; The Only Begotten Son; The True Messiah-Jesus Christ!

Psalm 148:13: "Let them praise the name of the Lord, for His name alone is exalted; His glory is above the earth and heaven."

Why?

Why did you stop encouraging
The ones I allowed to cross your path
Why did you stop being a witness
To those lost and confused suffering from life's wrath
Why did you stop feeling worthy of confessing My Name
Who hindered you, my child, the enemy is to blame
Why did you lose your boldness in Me only to open a door
for the enemy to come in and from his schemes you were
not strengthened to defend
Why did you lose your confidence for your righteousness is
in Me and no one else not even yourself from the devil's
trap you need to flee
Why did you lose your zeal in the Holy One only to believe
a lie that His promises He would not fulfill
Why did you lose your sensitivity to the Holy Spirit; I was
tugging on your heart but you weren't feeling it
Why did you get angry with God when all He was doing
was correcting you with the rod
Why did you choose to block out His voice
Why did you turn to another source
Why did you choose to stop studying and devouring God's
Word
Why did you stop praying for your voice He heard
Why did you stop fasting and seeking His face
All of this because you stepped out from under the Lord's
grace.
Then you lost your sense of worthiness though you were yet
covered in Jesus' righteousness!

My daughter/son, never lose connection with Me. No matter what you go through I am always there for you. I am life to all and the sustainer of all.

Why? (enlightened)

It is just an awesome feeling on the inside to know that you are living for Christ. Come what may, you are determined to stand and you know that if you have to fight in a spiritual battle, you already have your war clothes on and the enemy is in for the fight of the century. When you are confident, your spiritual heights rise to new levels. I do not mean being confident within you but in the greater one in you who is Christ. However, there is a flip side. You could become so distracted with the things of this world that you become stagnated in the things of Christ, and before long, you are wondering if salvation is still a part of you. You wonder and have scary thoughts like, if Christ would come today, would I still go back with Him? You stop witnessing, you stop praying, and the predicament becomes bigger than what it really has to be. How did you allow yourself to get so far away? How did your spirit become comatose to the things of God? You know you love God, but one thing led to another and the devil ended up trying to snatch you out of your Father's hands completely. You need to tell that devil he is a liar and you refuse to go back to the old way of life. God wants to know why you wandered off and left Him. He wants you to know that it does not matter; all you need to do is repent and ask Him to take you back. Do not worry about what other people have to say. They do not possess a hell or a heaven to place you in. God wants you back and that is all that matters. His love is too far beyond us to even comprehend. Do not make excuses of why you cannot turn back to God for there are more reasons to turn back than there are to stay as you are. God needs you to be His vessel of honor; come back home where you belong, God is waiting!

Psalm 86:5: "For you Lord, are good, and ready to forgive, and abundant in mercy to all those who call upon You."

Woe!

Woe! Unto those who have eyes, yet they cannot see that they are headed toward eternal damnation but that is not where God predestined them to be.

Woe! Unto those who have ears but cannot spiritually hear. For they have heard and are now hearing the salvation call of the Lord but yet they still do not have reverencing fear.

Woe! Unto those evildoers whose hands shed innocent blood. Repent and turn away for the wrath of God shall come among those like a mighty rushing flood.

Woe! Unto those who devise wicked schemes. Always plotting against another; beware for in hell you shall lift up your eyes and hear devastating screams.

Woe! Unto those who have tongues that lie! For you are allowing your mouth to sin and your soul must suffer when Jesus' judgment passes by.

Woe! Unto those who have quick evil feet! Can't you hear satan laughing at you loud and bold? He's laughing because he is slowly but surely conquering your soul.

Woe! Unto those who are always stirring up strife. For you are using the very weapon the enemy has given you to kill yourself...your own personal knife.

Woe! Unto those whose hearts are not pure. You adulterers, fornicators, hypocrites, witches, backbiters, gossipers, just to name a few. Your just reward is nigh and is soon to come upon you.

Woe! Unto those who blaspheme to say Jehovah God does not exist. You shall surely end up in the deepest of the abyss. Only a fool would say there is no God. How did you come to be? I do not give my God's glory to the big bang theory.

My God is alive and He is alive and well that is why I lift my voice and these words I tell. Hearken unto the voice of the Almighty God. Come out from among them who walk and do not do what is right. For Jesus is soon to come, just like a thief in the night, walking ever so gently to judge all our works by fire. And my prayer is that through this message you make heaven your home, that is truly my earnest desire.

He is standing waiting with His arms open wide.
Will you answer the call to stop your evil deeds and with Jesus abide?
The devil desires to sift you as wheat.
Turn the tables on him and make him end up in defeat.

The choice is yours,
He that has an ear let him hear what the spirit saith unto you!

Woe! (enlightened)

Woe means to stop suddenly and fasten your eyes on a particular thing, to watch out for danger ahead. God wants us to extensively examine every area in our lives. Are you giving God your best? He wants a thorough cleaning to take place today! Tomorrow may be too late! Stop playing around on the devil's territory! Give him all of his tools back. Give him back the tools of lying, cheating, stealing, profanity, backbiting, envy, lust, fornication, unfaithfulness, or whatever the tool is that he has been using to work in your life. Tell the devil that he is a liar and a deceiver and turn your back on him. You that are dibbling and dabbling in sin and talking against the things of God better know that judgment and damnation shall come. Run from the snare of the enemy. The Lord hates evil, but his ears are inclined to the righteous. Are you practicing evil or good?

Romans 6:12-14: "Therefore do not let sin reign in your mortal body, that you should obey it in its lusts. And do not present your members as instruments of unrighteousness to sin, but present yourselves to God as being alive from the dead, and your members as instruments of righteousness to God. For sin shall not have dominion over you, for you are not under law but under grace."

Women of Dominion

Pure, gentle, honest, and blessed
Walking in this world that we must possess.
Women have power more than they know.
They just have to use it and let the anointing of the Holy
Ghost flow.

Yes, we are the weaker vessel
Only in human strength.
But bless God, in the Spirit
We are powerful if the Holy Ghost we do not quench.

We need to walk in our authority
And let the great "I AM" be
That everyone in the world would know
It's not we ourselves but the Holy Ghost of power and
strength lives within me.

Women of God, rise up and take a stand.
Just remember to hold fast to God's unchanging hand.
We are powerful creatures, perfected and molded by God.
And can possess all things wherever our feet may trod.

So women of God, you vessels of honor, This I leave with
you
Consecrate yourselves,
Be pure, honest, and of noble character
But most of all, be TRUE!

Women of Dominion (enlightened)

There are a host of great women in the Bible, such as women who conquered great giants with the help of God. Some of the finest leaders in biblical times were women, and guess what, it does not stop there. Being a woman is not an easy job. It was only after God created "woman" that He rested. I like to say that He saved the best for last. I do not care who you are or what you may have been through, woman to woman, I want you to know that you are powerful, intelligent, and beautiful. It does not matter what your ethnicity may be; you are a well-designed creature and you are special in the sight of God. There are no duplicates of you. Stop making excuses for yourself. You are unique and no one else could ever do what you do. God loves you. He does not love the next one any more than He loves you. God made you the shape and color that you are and gave you a specific style that only you can be identified by. Who cares if others think you are strange? As long as you are using your God-given abilities to glorify God, keep on keeping on! Go and impact another woman's life today!

Galatians 3:28: "There is neither Jew nor Greek, there is neither male nor female; for you are all one in Christ Jesus."

Year of Jubilee

Hallelujah—Sing praises to our King
For this is our chosen year,
Go on and begin to sing!

Miraculous blessings He's getting ready to pour
Straight from the throne of grace
We are standing under an open door
He shall bind blessings to our lives that we shall
forever embrace
Showers of blessings I am being enabled to see
This is your year, the year of Jubilee.

Go free, all my children, your chains have been
destroyed
I have put the devil to shame
He is now unemployed

Rejoice you who were barren
The Word of God has set you free
Walk in your freedom, your divine Liberty

Great blessings await you
Align yourself that you may see
God's blessings raining in your life so abundantly

An overflow shall come, saith God
Have faith in Me!
Just move into the realm of the Spirit
And watch those devils flee

For those devils you use to see
You shall see no more
For God has given you the victory
You're standing under heaven's **open** door!

Year of Jubilee (enlightened)

We've been waiting long enough! We have stood the test of time! We have endured hardship. We have been troubled on every side, yet we are still here. God is getting ready to blow your mind! People are going to look at you and say, "That had to be God!" God is getting ready, and as a matter of fact, He is beginning to work out some things in your life right now as you read this exhorted word! You have been through a lot and have remained faithful. God is getting ready to flood your life with the things you've been praying for. Everything that the devil has tampered with in your life God is getting ready to restore. This is a faith word. You know where you are, and you know what you have been through. Get ready for this awesome move of God in your life. He is getting ready to re-establish major letdowns and disappointments. He is restoring health to the sick, freedom to the oppressed, prosperity to the poor, faith to the doubters, miracles for the believers, salvation to the unsaved, and He is releasing the wealth of the wicked to the upright! Get ready to receive your miracle according to your faith. Allow this word to be deposited in your spirit. I can only expound on what God has put in my spirit to give to His people. It is up to you to receive it. This is your year, and I touch and agree with every believer who knows this truth that supernatural doors are being opened and the devil has already been put to flight! Shout with a loud voice so that you shake the very gates of hell—RESTORATION! Now begin to thank God for restoring your marriage, your finances, your health, and your mind! All you need is the faith of a mustard seed and it's yours! No tricks, no gimmicks—just believe!

Joel 2:25-27: "So I will restore to you the years that the swarming locust has eaten, the crawling locust, the consuming locust, and the chewing locust, My great army which I sent among you. You shall eat in plenty and be satisfied, and praise and praise the name of the Lord your God, who has dealt wondrously with you; and My people shall never be put to shame. Then you shall know that I am in the midst of Israel (my people) I am the Lord your God and there is no other. My people will never be put to shame."

Yes, I Have Risen but Have I Risen in You?

Everyone wants to tell the story
How Jesus died, was buried, and rose
Yet you have not too many that testify
Of how He got up and redeemed their souls.

We all know Jesus rose
He is alive and well
Yet how many of us can say He has also
risen on the inside and we are not destined for hell?

Can you witness to His saving grace?
Can you tell the story of His warm embrace?
How you were once a wretch in sin
But you allowed Jesus to arise within.

He was beaten badly, nails were put in His hands and
feet; He was spit upon, beard pulled from his face
All because of His love for us
That we might be joint heirs with Him and abide under
His amazing grace

Jesus loved us so He died with agonizing pain
For you not to accept Him
Is like saying He died in vain

Some of us may say
We do live for Him
But the light we reflect on the inside
Is very shallow and dim

Our spiritual walk is as the world
and our talk has not changed
No one can see the transformation
That on the inside Jesus reigns.

We walk around and talk a good talk
And it sounds good to the ear
But only God alone knows wholeheartedly
If our walk and talk is truly sincere.

Resurrection Day what does it really mean to you?
Just one day out of the year to show up for church
For that is what tradition tells us to do.

To me it is the day
To reflect back on how Jesus set us free
How He became a curse for us
For it was not you but Him that hung upon a tree.

Do you live a life worthy of the Savior
That was wounded for our transgressions and bruised
for our iniquities
Or are you still crucifying Him
By not accepting Him and going on with your lifeless
deeds?

Today is your day of decision
Harden not your heart
For Jesus has done all He's going to do
It's up to you to do your part

I offer you Jesus, The Prince of Peace,
Who is faithful and true
For He has without a doubt risen
but I ask you again has He risen in you?

Yes, I Have Risen (enlightened)

Have you ever met anyone who wants you to think they "got it going on" with Christ? They say all the religious sayings and they try to act in such a "holy" way. They do not want you to know them for who they really are for some are such counterfeit Christians that when it's time for the tire to meet the road in their lives, you see that they were just blowing smoke. They will "cuss" you out just as quickly as they look at you. They will tell you about yourself and your momma, but just as soon as the church doors are open, they are the first ones up out-shouting everyone else. Does this mean that Christians are perfect, and they do not have issues? No, of course not. All I am saying is be real in all that you do and allow others to see where you have missed it in life and where you sometimes continue to miss it. Be true to God and yourself. Stop walking around trying to work your way into heaven. The way has already been made for you. Stop spending countless hours out of the day performing in your walk with Christ and face up to the areas where you need help. God wants to rise in your heart, to clean all the filthiness out so that He may replace it with His love and peace. Faking it will never allow you to make it. God wants you to tell Him about your hang-ups (though He already knows) and ask for sincere help from Him. Then once you get what you need, you can always go back and help someone who is going through some of the same trials that you have been faced with yourself. Jesus wants to be transparent in your life. He wants you to be a living testimony for Him. He has already completed the work. All you have to do is accept all that He has done for you. Let God arise on the inside, allow yourself to do a 180-degree turn, and allow God to change you from the inside out. Are you ready to allow God to rise in you and become a true follower of Christ?

Matthew 15:7-9: "Hypocrites! Well did Isaiah prophesy about you, saying: These people draw near to Me with their mouth, and honor Me with their lips, but their heart is far from Me. And in vain they worship Me, teaching as doctrines the commandments of men."

Your Tongue Must Die

We talk and we talk
Not even knowing why
But today, at this very hour
I'm here to tell you, your tongue must die.

We try to go forth in worship
and then try to praise
Yet, these are the very ones
That continuously have confusion raised

You have no power or life
God's strength of yours has now gone
Think back to where you lost it
I know, sitting around gossiping on the telephone.

Stop your lifeless deeds
For you are slowly losing your soul
Please don't end up in hell
For some unfruitful seeds you've sowed.

God said, "Get rid of that deadly poison"
And it's not in your own strength, so don't try
Take heed of my words, your tongue must die.

In denial you say, "Oh, it's just a test"
No child, no, it's that your tongue needs rest.
You are cursing yourself, can't you see how
Ask God to help you crucify that tongue
Then it shall die.

Your Tongue Must Die (enlightened)

Have you ever taken the time to notice that God gave us two eyes, two ears, two hands, and two feet? He even sent his disciples out by twos, but He only gave us one mouth. What an awesome God. For if He had given some of us two mouth-pieces, we would have talked ourselves straight to hell from the very beginning. God knew that we only needed one mouth and sometimes that one is more than enough! Our mouths, in one breath, can bless our God, lifting Him up and glorifying His Name, and in the next breath, curse our fellow men and women who are made in the very likeness of God. This is not pleasing in the sight of God. If your words do not line up with the Word of God, then I ask you a question: Who are you allowing to control you? It is going to take the power of the Holy Spirit to keep your mouth from being boastful and unruly. You cannot do it without God's help. Do not permit your tongue to spark fires by word of mouth that ruins relationships within your family, within your church, on your job, and especially within your house. Put your mouth to use and begin to encourage other believers in the faith. Go out and witness about your Lord and Savior! Go and tell someone how special he or she is to you. Exhort, encourage, and comfort all men and women for we are all God's children.

James 3:6: "And the tongue is a fire, a world of iniquity. The tongue is so set among our members that it defiles the whole body, and sets on fire the course of nature; and it is set on fire by hell."

Printed in the United States
55633LVS00004B/535-645

9 781418 445355